CHRIS JERICHO

BY JASON BRICKWEG

BELLWETHER MEDIA • MINNEAPOLIS, MN

Are you ready to take it to the extreme?
Torque books thrust you into the action-packed world
of sports, vehicles, mystery, and adventure. These books
may include dirt, smoke, fire, and dangerous stunts.
WARNING: read at your own risk.

Library of Congress Cataloging-in-Publication Data

Brickweg, Jason.
  Chris Jericho / by Jason Brickweg.
     p. cm. -- (Torque: Pro wrestling champions)
  Includes bibliographical references and index.
  Summary: "Engaging images accompany information about Chris Jericho. The combination of
high-interest subject matter and light text is intended for students in grades 3 through 7"--Provided by
publisher.
  ISBN 978-1-60014-902-3 (hardcover : alk. paper)
1. Jericho, Chris--Juvenile literature. 2. Wrestlers--Canada--Biography--Juvenile literature. I. Title.
GV1196.J47B75 2013
796.812092--dc23
[B]   2012042320

This edition first published in 2013 by Bellwether Media, Inc.

Printed in the United States of America, North Mankato, MN.

The images in this book are reproduced through the courtesy of: Devin Chen, front cover, pp. 12-13,
15, 16-17; LatinContent/Getty Images, pp. 4-5; FOREST LUGH/FEATURECHINA /Newscom, p. 7;
WireImage, p. 8; Zuma Press, pp. 9, 14, 18; CD1 WENN Photos/Newscom, pp. 10-11; Getty Images,
p. 18; Chris Ryan/Corbis/APImages, pp. 18-19; Associated Press, pp. 20-21.

CONTENTS

WARNING!

The wrestling moves used in this book are performed
by professionals. Do not attempt to reenact any
of the moves performed in this book.

NINE-TIME CHAMPION

A **No Holds Barred Match** had moved outside the ring at Extreme Rules 2009. Chris Jericho and Rey Mysterio were wrestling for the Intercontinental Championship. The two battled on the arena floor. Then they brought the action back to the ring.

REY
MYSTERIO

VITAL STATS

Wrestling Name: _____ Chris Jericho

Real Name: _____ Christopher Keith Irvine

Height: _____ 6 feet (1.8 meters)

Weight: _____ 226 pounds (103 kilograms)

Started Wrestling: _____ 1990

Finishing Move: _____ Codebreaker

Jericho tried to hit Mysterio with a metal chair. Mysterio used a **dropkick** to protect himself. Soon he had Jericho hanging off the ropes. It was the perfect setup for a **619**. However, Jericho stopped it and tore Mysterio's mask from his face. He made the pin and won his ninth Intercontinental Championship!

WHO IS CHRIS JERICHO?

Christopher Keith Irvine was born on November 9, 1970 in Manhasset, New York. He spent most of his childhood in Manitoba, Canada. Sports were a big part of his youth. Irvine was an **all-around athlete**. He was also the son of a professional hockey player.

Irvine became interested in wrestling at a young age. He watched matches on television with his grandmother and also attended shows. Irvine met wrestling stars Ricky Steamboat and Jesse Ventura when he was a teenager. They inspired him to follow in their footsteps.

At age 19, Irvine moved to Calgary to attend wrestling school. He **debuted** in the Canadian **independent circuit** a couple months later. Then he wrestled in Mexico, Germany, Japan, and the United States. Irvine's success caught the attention of World Wrestling Entertainment (WWE).

QUICK HIT!

"Cowboy" Chris Jericho teamed up with Lance Storm in the Canadian independent circuit.

BECOMING A CHAMPION

In 1999, Jericho debuted as "Y2J" in WWE. He claimed to be its savior. That year he defeated Chyna to win his first Intercontinental Championship. Jericho started a **feud** with Chris Benoit in 2000. It later turned into a partnership. At the end of 2001, Jericho did something that had never been done. He held two WWE championships at the same time!

Jericho and Christian wrestled as a **tag team** for a while. Their partnership ended in a feud. In 2005, Jericho left WWE. He returned two years later and soon won his eighth Intercontinental Championship. In 2009, he claimed the title for the ninth time. Then he and Big Show teamed up. They had a 140-day **reign** as Tag Team Champions.

BIG
SHOW

QUICK HIT!

Jericho is the lead singer of a heavy metal band. He leaves WWE for short periods of time to tour.

Jericho has a unique collection of **signature moves**. WWE fans know him for the Walls of Jericho and the Lionsault. For the Walls of Jericho, he grabs an opponent by the legs and holds him upside down. Then Jericho turns the opponent facedown and sits on him. The Lionsault is a backflip off the ropes and onto the opponent.

LIONSAULT

CODEBREAKER

finishing move. He grabs an opponent's head and brings his knees to the wrestler's face. Then he falls backward onto the mat. This forces the opponent to slam into his knees. The Codebreaker helps Jericho continue to be a record-breaker in WWE!

QUICK HIT!

Jericho is a Grand Slam Champion. He earned this title by winning four different WWE championships.

GLOSSARY

519—a move in which a wrestler swings between the second and third ropes to hit an opponent on the ropes

all-around athlete—an athlete who is skilled at many different sports

debuted—first appeared

dropkick—a move in which a wrestler jumps and then kicks an opponent with both feet

feud—a long-lasting, heated rivalry between two people or teams

finishing move—a wrestling move meant to finish off an opponent so that he can be pinned

independent circuit—the minor league of professional wrestling

No Holds Barred Match—a wrestling match that allows the use of weapons and outside interference; a wrestler cannot be disqualified from a No Holds Barred Match.

reign—the time during which a person holds a title or position of power

signature moves—moves that a wrestler is famous for performing

tag team—two wrestlers who compete as a team

TO LEARN MORE

AT THE LIBRARY

Black, Jake. *The Ultimate Guide to WWE*. New York, N.Y.: Grosset & Dunlap, 2011.

Brickweg, Jason. *Christian*. Minneapolis, Minn.: Bellwether Media, 2013.

Price, Sean Stewart. *The Kids' Guide to Pro Wrestling*. Mankato, Minn.: Edge Books, 2012.

ON THE WEB

Learning more about Chris Jericho is as easy as 1, 2, 3.

1. Go to www.factsurfer.com.

2. Enter "Chris Jericho" into the search box.

3. Click the "Surf" button and you will see a list of related Web sites.

With factsurfer.com, finding more information

INDEX